CW00402552

LOADING THEODORE ROOSEVELT'S SAFARI SUPPLIES, NEW YORK, 1909

THE PLEASURES OF SAFARI ADVENTURE

A Pavilion Companion

Introduction

Safari in Swahili literally means a journey, but is now widely interpreted to mean an adventurous holiday, observing wild animals. Today, this ranges from tailor-made luxury to mass tourism in zebra-striped mini-buses. In earlier days, however, going "on safari" hinted at a certain wild glamour, combining, as it did, danger and excitement with the comforting sociability of swapping yarns around a camp fire at sundown, or the exhilaration of dining out under a miraculous canopy of stars.

The change from actually hunting big game to merely observing through the camera lens has been gradual, but as early as 1899, a former African governor described Edward North Buxton as, "having the courage to stand before a snobbish public and proclaim that the best sport for a man of cultured mind is the snapshooting with a camera rather than the pumping of lead into elephants, rhinoceroses, antelopes, zebras and many other harmless, beautiful or rare beasts and birds."

That did not deter the many who descended on East Africa in the early half of the century, primarily game hunters or pioneer settlers. Initially, game hunting was an elite sport for a privileged few, but gradually word spread that here was a unique experience.

Famous safaris were those of Churchill, Theodore Roosevelt, the Duke of Connaught, and the Prince of Wales (later to abdicate as Edward VIII), accompanied by such legendary hunters as Denys Finch Hatton, Bror Blixen and Philip Percival. Some of these are enshrined for posterity in Karen Blixen's or Hemingway's classic writings about Africa, but other first-hand accounts can make amusing reading. In the 1920s, the work of pioneer film-makers and photographers, Martin and Osa Johnson, brought the mysteries of animal behaviour to a wider audience.

The original "safaris" were led by qualified hunters whose expert knowledge of animals and terrain was literally a life-saver. Clientele developed from the original elite of dukes, princes, politicians and aristocrats, to financiers, movie-stars and other would-be adventurers. New companies emerged for organisation and equipment, as the large safaris needed quantities of provisions and tenting, food, and portable bathrooms, often for many months on end.

Hunting has always been carefully controlled and licensed under the jurisdiction of the Game Departments, but in some countries where hunting is banned, as in Kenya in 1977, this has actually encouraged the poachers to greater illegal activity. One must wonder which is more beneficial to the balance of nature. The game conservancy debate will continue to rage as species dwindle.

A journey to Africa is not only a geographical journey, but a journey of self-discovery. For nowhere in the northern hemisphere can one experience such a vast expanse of sky and land. It is both overwhelming and humbling to see landscape on such a vast scale: one feels smaller than an ant on the face of infinity. Faced with this, companionship is a boon to some, as reassurance, but to others, it is that particular peace and isolation found only in the bush that is the essential ingredient of a safari.

The combination of wild beauty and danger tinged with fear produces a form of adrenalin too rarely met in daily urban life. These elements of safari are no less vivid today but man is sadly encroaching on this natural paradise. However, to paraphrase Isak Dinesen, once you feel the "rhythm of Africa" you are *hooked*. Nothing can equal the thrill of seeing your first lion in the wild. Nothing can replace the fascination of watching a lioness feeding her cubs, or the sight of that first elephant. In the latter half of the twentieth century, when we are spoilt with film and television bringing the world to us, there is still nothing to equal the real safari adventure.

Jenny de Gex, 1991

African Paradise

The land teems with beasts of the chase, infinite in number and incredible in variety. It holds the fiercest beasts of ravin, and the fleetest and most timid of those things that live in undying fear of talon and fang. It holds the largest and the smallest of hoofed animals. It holds the mightiest creatures that tread the earth or swim in its rivers; it also holds distant kinsfolk of these same creatures, no bigger than woodchucks, which dwell in crannies of the rocks, and in the tree-tops. There are antelope smaller than hares, and antelope larger than oxen. There are creatures which are the embodiments of grace; and others whose huge ungainliness is like that of a shape in a nightmare. The plains are alive with droves of strange and beautiful animals whose like is not known elsewhere; and with others, even stranger, that show both in form and temper something of the fantastic and the grotesque. It is a never-ending pleasure to gaze at the great herds of buck as they move to and fro in their myriads; as they stand for their noontide rest in the quivering heat haze; as the long files come down to drink at the watering-places; as they feed and fight and rest and make love.

African Game Trails, Theodore Roosevelt, 1910

The Pioneers

There was always a stir of excitement in Nairobi when the old porter safaris left. They could form a mile-long string as eighty to a hundred of them, bearing head-loads, left for the bush with a small knot of white men, the clients and hunters, bringing up the rear.

Originally the term 'white' hunter referred to a sportsman whose colour of skin singled him out from the Africans, the amateur who stalked and shot game by his own prowess. It may be apochryphal but there is a plausible story that the term originated through Alan Black, who, even in 1907, was much respected as a 'white hunter'.

Scion of a distinguished line of clipper captains, Black took French leave from school to join in the Boer War, and by the age of seventeen, in 1903, had investigated settling in Nairobi. Delamere needed two hunters to shoot game for his porters (possibly when he was immobilised from his fall on the Athi Plains) and employed Alan Black whose skill at shooting with a bow and arrow was as great as that with a gun. But the second hunter was a Somali who also acted as *Neapara* or headman in camp. To differentiate between the two, on account of Black's surname, the Somali was referred to as 'the black hunter' while Black was always called 'the white hunter' and from this circumstance, the term caught on and stuck.

At any rate for the first time in Africa's history the role of white hunter was created, romanticised and then glamorized. More often than not, full-time professional hunters emerged gradually out of the ordinary pioneer farmer who shot well and was attempting to earn extra income.

The Kenya Pioneers, Errol Trzebinski, 1985

AFRICAN ADVENTURES, 1890

"I Speak of Africa..."

"I speak of Africa and golden joys"; the joy of wandering through lonely lands; the joy of hunting the mighty and terrible lords of the wilderness, the cunning, the wary, and the grim.

In these greatest of the world's great hunting-grounds there are mountain-peaks whose snows are dazzling under the equatorial sun; swamps where the slime oozes and bubbles and festers in the steaming heat; lakes like seas; skies that burn above deserts where the iron desolation is shrouded from view by the wavering mockery of the mirage; vast grassy plains where palms and thorn-trees fringe the dwindling streams; mighty rivers rushing out of the heart of the continent through the sadness of endless marshes; forests of gorgeous beauty, where death broods in the dark and silent depths.

African Game Trails, Theodore Roosevelt, 1910

A Swahili Word

That is how the story of my *safari* begins (*safari* is a Swahili word meaning expedition; it is noun and verb and adjective all in one). The story is a long one and an exciting one. It is exciting not only because it tells of narrow escapes. We had narrow escapes, Osa and I, but it is not for that we are going back to Africa. We are going back because we love the land and we love the animals. As for excitement, you may live in what I call excitement from the moment you first look out of your tent in the morning until you lie in your cot at night, listening to the night sounds – the hollow, terrifying roar of the lion, the bark of the zebra, the ghostly laugh of the hyena, and the *pad*, *pad* of invisible feet.

Camera Trails in Africa, Martin Johnson, 1924

THE SAFARI GETS UNDERWAY FOR LAKE PARADISE

IN THE EARLY DAYS

Ox-wagons for the next stage of our journey were waiting for us in charge of a Boer settler. They were cumbersome, springless affairs, with hooded tops, looking much like the prairie-schooners of our own pioneer West. Each was drawn by six oxen, and was capable, so we were told, of a speed of about fifteen miles a day. Fortunately, our destination was less than a day's ride distant.

We were off betimes next morning, so as to be sure to arrive before nightfall. We set off in the dark, and went creaking and rattling off into the plains. Osa and Dad and I rode in the Fords. Our boys plodded alongside. The Boer, a man so phlegmatic and slow that he seemed to us half-imbecile, drove one of the wagons; the other was driven by a native boy. Each driver had a *voor-looper* or fore-runner who led the front span of oxen by means of a strip of rawhide attached to their horns. Once in the driver's seat, the Boer came to life. From being a moron, he became a maniac, for the driver of an ox-wagon in Africa combines the methods of a ring-master in a circus and a cheer-leader at a college football game.

Camera Trails in Africa, Martin Johnson, 1924

Of Man and Lion

Man is still a hunter, still a simple searcher after meat for his growling belly, still a provider for his helpless mate and cubs. Else why am I here? From the moment he wakes until the moment he closes his eyes, man's prime concern is the business of making a living for himself and his family. *Bringing home the bacon* is the modern equivalent of banging a curly mammoth over the head with a big sharp rock.

Man has found it exceedingly difficult lately to decipher the weird incantations and ceremonies which surround the provision of meat and shelter for his spawn. He is mystified by the cabalistic signs of the economist. He does not understand billions of dollars in relationship to him and his. Parity baffles him; the administration of ceilings and floors and controls and excises and supports does not satisfy his meat urge or his aesthetic response to the chase, when the hunter's horn of necessity rouses him. *These are pretty fine thoughts*, I thought. *I will think some more.*

But he can understand a lion, because a lion is life in its simplest form, beautiful, menacing, dangerous, and attractive to his ego. A lion has always been the symbol of challenge, the prototype of personal hazard. You get the lion or the lion gets you.

Horn of the Hunter, Robert C. Ruark, 1954

ON THE GAME TRAIL

The White Hunter

The popular conception of a white hunter, built largely in the American mind on film portrayals by Gregory Peck and Stewart Granger, is almost as erroneous as the movie and popular magazine accounts of African safaris. According to what you may have seen or read, the basic idea of a professional hunter is roughly this:

He stands about six foot five, sports a full beard, and is drunk (off his client's liquor) most of the time. He always makes a play for the client's beautiful wife and/or sister, and always scores. He shoots lions with pistols and wrestles with snakes and buffalo for fun. When he is not out on safari he hangs around bars in Nairobi, ogling the girls and thumbing the big cartridges he wears in the loops of his jacket. He does all the shooting for the client, while the client sits comfortably in the shooting car. He is always taciturn in a me-Tarzan-you-Jane manner. He has a secret sorrow which drove him to a life among the wild beasts. His business is regarded as butchery, and it takes a superhuman man to be a competent butcher.

This is about as accurate as the average movie presentation of high life in New York, or the general supposition that all Englishmen have no chins and sport monocles.

Horn of the Hunter, Robert C. Ruark, 1954

Reflections of a Hunter

Now it is pleasant to hunt something that you want very much over a long period of time, being outwitted, out-manoeuvred, and failing at the end of each day, but having the hunt and knowing every time you are out that, sooner or later, your luck will change and that you will get the chance that you are seeking. But it is not pleasant to have a time limit by which you must get your kudu or perhaps never get it, nor even see one. It is not the way hunting should be. It is too much like those boys who used to be sent to Paris with two years in which to make good as writers or painters, after which, if they had not made good, they could go home and into their fathers' businesses. The way to hunt is for as long as you live against as long as there is such and such an animal; just as the way to paint is as long as there is you and colours and canvas, and to write as long as you can live and there is pencil and paper or ink or any machine to do it with, or anything you care to write about, and you feel a fool, and you are a fool, to do it any other way.

Green Hills of Africa, Ernest Hemingway, 1936

PHILIP PERCIVAL AND ERNEST HEMINGWAY ON SAFARI, 1933

Night Sounds

I remember how the fire looked that night, and the flicker of the smaller fires on the shining black faces of the boys as they squatted round, roasting their bits of meat. I remember how marvellous the warm martinis tasted, and that we had eland chops for dinner, and we drank far too much brandy afterwards as we sat in front of the fire in robes and pyjamas, saying the same triumphant things to each other over and over again. I remember how the boys grabbed me by the thumb in that queer handshake of theirs when we came in with the second lion, and the almost reverent light in old Katunga's mad eyes as he ran his thumb across the blade of his skinning knife, looking first at the red-headed lion, then at me.

"*M'uzuri sana, bwana,*" old Katunga said. "*M'kubwa sana. M'uzuri, m'uzuri. Piga m'zuri. Bwana Simbambile.*"

It sounded very fine to be called Bwana Two Lions that night, which is maybe why I am today dissatisfied with cocktail conversation and stale talk of politics and football scandals and congressional investigations. Also, my taste in sports has been somewhat spoiled.

This was a very fine *simba*, this last lion that I shall ever shoot. He had this real red mane, as red as Ann Sheridan's, and bright green eyes. He was absolutely prime, not an ounce of fat on him, no sores, few flies, with a fine shining healthy coat. He was the handsomest lion I had ever seen, in or out of a zoo, and I was not sorry about the collection of him. Already I was beginning to fall into the African way of thinking: that if you properly respect what you are after, and shoot it cleanly and on the animal's terrain, if you imprison in your mind all the wonder of the day from sky to smell to breeze to flowers – then you have not merely killed an animal. You have lent immortality to a beast you have killed because you loved him and wanted him for ever so that you could always recapture the day.

Horn of the Hunter, Robert C. Ruark, 1954

The Prince of Wales on Safari

Meantime H.R.H., Finch Hatton and Salmon had walked east. They intended to camp on the Tangi River (a tributary of the Victoria Nile) and there search for elephants or anything else. They took with them a safari of porters. 'Safari', a word that appears on many pages in this book, is a Swahili word and, like many other words in the Swahili language, comes from the Arabic. It means literally 'a journey'. But its uses are liberal. It may mean a hunting trip, it may be applied, coupled with the verb 'make', to African sport generally (much, but not quite, as the word 'shikar' is applied in the East). It may mean a string of black porters who carry a prince's kit or a bagman's samples.

Porters have advantages over pack animals. They do not stray, nor do they get sore backs. And they can go anywhere. But they are sometimes temperamental *en masse* and they sometimes go on strike, generally because they are not getting enough game meat to go with their porridge. They are in charge of a headman, a native who is responsible to his white employer for the discipline and morals of his men. But a hundred men, black or white, require handling with tact.

Sport and Travel in East Africa, compiled from the diaries of the Prince of Wales,
Patrick Chalmers, 1934

DENYS FINCH HATTON WITH HIS CLIENT EDWARD, PRINCE OF WALES (RIGHT) AND GAMEWARDEN JOCK AIRD. THE HUNTING PARTY STOPPED FOR TEA EVERY AFTERNOON AT 4.00 O'CLOCK.

Sighting Buffalo

Out on the safaris, I had seen a herd of buffalo, one hundred and twenty-nine of them, come out of the morning mist under a copper sky, one by one, as if the dark and massive, iron-like animals with the mighty horizontally swung horns were not approaching, but were being created before my eyes and sent out as they were finished. I had seen a herd of elephant travelling through the dense native forest, where the sunlight is strewn down between the thick creepers in small spots and patches, pacing along as if they had an appointment at the end of the world. It was, in giant size, the border of a very old, infinitely precious Persian carpet, in the dyes of green, yellow, and black-brown. I had time after time watched the progression across the plain of the giraffe, in their queer, inimitable, vegetative gracefulness, as if it were not a herd of animals but a family of rare, long-stemmed, speckled gigantic flowers slowly advancing. I had followed two rhinos on their morning promenade, when they were sniffing and snorting in the air of the dawn – which is so cold that it hurts in the nose – and looked like two very big angular stones rollicking in the long valley and enjoying life together. I had seen the royal lion, before sunrise, below a waning moon, crossing the grey plain on his way home from the kill, drawing a dark wake in the silvery grass, his face still red up to the ears, or during the midday siesta, when he reposed contentedly in the midst of his family on the short grass and in the delicate, spring-like shade of the broad acacia trees of his park of Africa.

Out of Africa, Karen Blixen, 1937

Stars and Stripes

As a compliment, which I much appreciated, a large American flag was floating over my own tent; and in the front line, flanking this tent on either hand, were other big tents for the members of the party, with a dining tent and a skinning tent; while behind were the tents of the two hundred porters, the gun-bearers, the tent-boys, the askaris, or native soldiers, and the horse-boys, or saises. In front of the tents stood the men in two lines, the first containing the fifteen askaris, the second the porters with their head-men. The askaris were uniformed, each in a red fez, a blue blouse, and white knickerbockers, and each carrying his rifle and belt. The porters were chosen from several different tribes or races, to minimize the danger of combination in the event of mutiny.

Here and there in East Africa one can utilize ox-waggons or pack-trains of donkeys; but for a considerable expedition it is still best to use a safari of native porters, of the type by which the commerce and exploration of the country have always been carried on.

African Game Trails, Theodore Roosevelt, 1910

Mr Roosevelt's and Kermit's camp near which they got the rhino and elephant

The Eternal Elephant

Elephant-hunting is a sport of its own. For the elephant, which through centuries has been the one head of game hunted for profit, in the course of time has adopted man into his scheme of things, with deep distrust. Our nearness to him is a challenge which he will never disregard; he comes towards us, straightly and quickly, on his own, a towering, overwhelming structure, massive as cast iron and lithe as running water. 'What time he lifteth up himself on high, the mighty are afraid.' Out go his ears like a dragon's wings, giving him a grotesque likeness to the small lap-dog called a papillon; his formidable trunk, crumpled up accordion-like, rises above us like a lifted scourge. There is passion in our meeting, positiveness on both sides; but on his side there is no pleasure in the adventure, he is driven on by just wrath, and is settling an ancient family feud.

In very old days the elephant, upon the roof of the earth, led an existence deeply satisfying to himself and fit to be set up as an example to the rest of creation: that of a being mighty and powerful beyond anyone's attack, attacking no one.

"Barua A Soldani", *Shadows in the Grass*, Isak Dinesen, (Karen Blixen), 1960

Life Under Canvas

I am always amazed when I think of how much living can be compressed into a tent settlement. We had four major tents, not counting the toilet one. We had a big double-fly job for the *memsaab* and the *bwana*. Selby slept in a single double-fly. There was a big open-faced dining tent in which all the boxes of food were stacked. There was a tiny cook tent, and some of the boys had shelter-halves. It takes fifty minutes to set it all up, and the next day it bears the earmarks of a thriving city. Somehow it suddenly becomes logical to go to the john in a canvas cell and to wash your dirty body in a canvas coffin, in water full of living things, and to sleep soundly with the hyenas tripping over the tent ropes.

The sounds become wonderfully important. There is a dove that sounds like a goosed schoolgirl. He says: "Oooh. Oooh! *OOOHH!*" The bush babies cry. The colobus monkeys snort like lions, except it does not carry the implied threat. At first it is hard to tell the baboons from the leopards when they curse each other in a series of guttural grunts. A hyena can roar like a lion. A lion mostly mutters with an asthmatic catch in his throat. The insects are tumultuous. A well-situated jungle camp is not quiet. But the noise makes itself into a pattern which is soothing except when the hyenas start to giggle. A hyena's giggle is date night in the female ward of a madhouse.

Horn of the Hunter, Robert C. Ruark, 1954

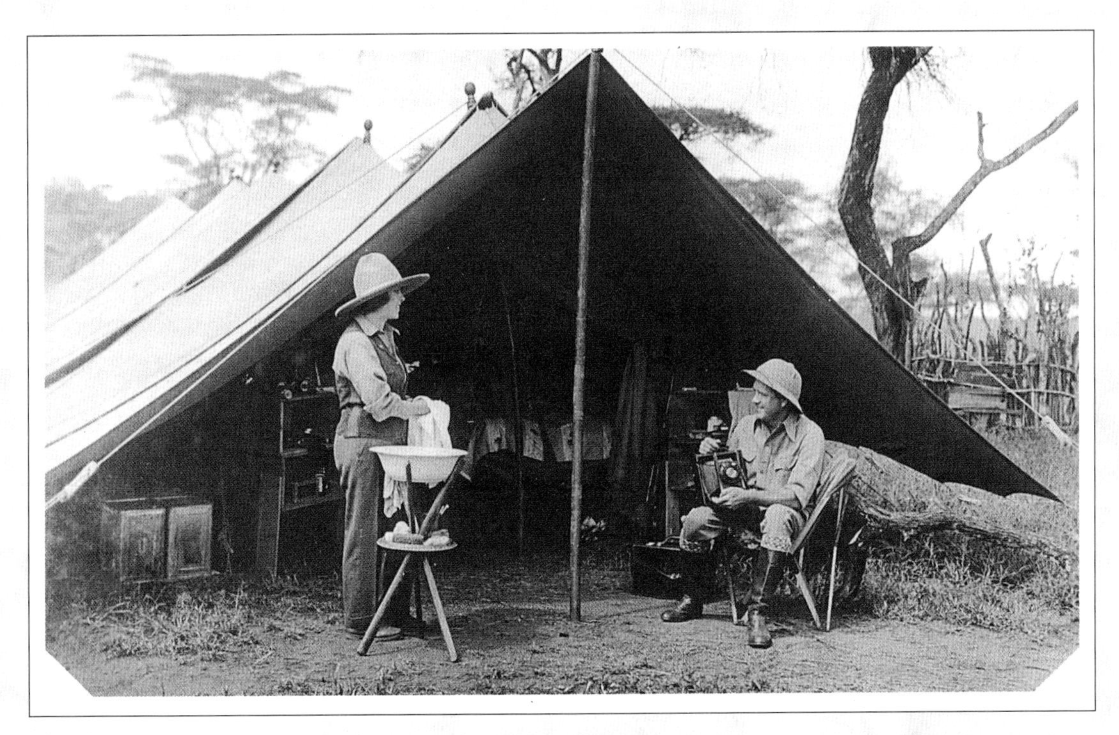

In front of our home in Tanganyika.

Osa got so used to wearing trousers that she said she afterwards felt self-conscious when she had to wear dresses in civilisation. Note the tent inside with the fly over it.

Zebras in the Sun

And the animals! Can you imagine a parched brown plain rolling off to a deep blue line against a turquoise sky, and in the foreground a group of zebras drinking from a pool that is gold in the afternoon sun – perfect little horses, elegantly striped in black and white, smooth and glossy as if they had been curried, quick and graceful in movement as an Arab mare? Can you imagine a herd of giraffes feeding among the gray-green thorny mimosas, animals eighteen feet tall, their deep burnt-orange hides covered with an irregular network of white lines? Can you imagine ugly rhinos snorting like great angry pigs in the night just outside your hut of stones and thorn-bush? You look out and see them, big as motor-cars, their gray hides turned to white by the moon, and their horns looking even wickeder than they look in daytime. You throw a stone to frighten them off, for they might with a movement send your hut rolling down on top of you, and two of them grow angry and rush at each other head down. They send great stones crashing down the hill as they struggle together. Can you imagine beautiful fawn-colored gazelles, with great soft eyes and long, gracefully curved ringed horns, stepping lightly down to drink at a water-hole? When they pass a clump of grasses, they break into a run for fear of the lion that may be lying in wait for them. Can you imagine waiting for King Lion himself to come to feed on the zebra you have killed as bait for him, and seeing him at last after hours of suspense – not the moth-eaten, stupefied lion of the zoo, but a free animal with healthy skin and mane, and an easy step, and live muscles that play visibly under his hide? He vaguely suspects your presence and looks about suspiciously and emits a hollow roar to show that he is not to be trifled with. Can you imagine yourself unexpectedly face to face with a great African elephant whose tusks are longer than a man is tall and whose ears are big enough for the sides of a pup-tent?

Camera Trails in Africa, Martin Johnson, 1924

On The Move

When we were to march, camp was broken as early in the day as possible. Each man had his allotted task, and the tents, bedding, provisions, and all else were expeditiously made into suitable packages. Each porter is supposed to carry from fifty-five to sixty pounds, which may all be in one bundle or in two or three. The American flag, which flew over my tent, was a matter of much pride to the porters, and was always carried at the head or near the head of the line of march; and after it in single file came the long line of burden-bearers. As they started, some of them would blow on horns or whistles, and others beat little tom-toms; and at intervals this would be renewed again and again throughout the march; or the men might suddenly begin to chant, or merely to keep repeating in unison some one word or one phrase which, when we asked to have it translated, might or might not prove to be entirely meaningless. The headmen carried no burdens, and the tent-boys hardly anything, while the saises walked with the spare horses.

African Game Trails, Theodore Roosevelt, 1910

Breaking Camp

The Height of the Giraffe

While on this topic of giraffe and trains, I may as well notice the other point of collision between giraffe and civilisation – the telegraph wires. Twenty years ago, or thereabout, complaints arising out of damaged lines were many. I used to receive plaintive messages from the gentleman responsible for the telegraphs, saying he should like to know what I would propose to do. "Either you must keep your giraffe off the lines or we shall have to raise them," was the way he put it. I was sorry for the man, but we were in the same boat: officially speaking, the giraffe were mine, as he said, and the telegraph lines were his. Government wants both giraffe and telegraph lines, and I am afraid it lies with the telegraph man to solve the difficulty: he can raise his lines, whereas the Game Department can't shorten its giraffe.

These troubles occur, as a rule, in the bush country, and when the giraffe are travelling at a leisurely pace; for when going at speed through bush the head is carried low to avoid trees and branches, which is done with wonderful skill and adroitness. The telegraph wires generally come off second best, but exceptions occur.

A Game Ranger's Notebook, A. Blayney-Percival, 1925

Boy-Scouts

One of the Waccoma chiefs took a great fancy to the Boy-Scouts. He stands here on an ant-hill pointing out to them a nearby Donga in which he declares they will find lions. The chief was right.

Lion, Martin Johnson, 1929

THE CHIEF POINTS THE WAY

"An Awful Lot of God . . ."

We drove slowly back to the old Bowman camp-site, watching the game and hearing the noises and feeling the sun still warm as the breeze stiffened and grew chillier, as content as seven white and black people can be. We stopped for another look at the camp, and as we walked into it another young kudu bull barked, leaped, and streaked across the ground on which we would be living tomorrow. The shady grove still looked like a cathedral. We walked to the river again, and the same crocodiles looked bored and slid into the stream. The same elephants, I suppose, bugled across in the deep green thicket across the way. There were two or three other piles of fresh dung, deposited since we had left that morning.

"You know," Selby said, "I am not a particularly religious man, but there's an awful lot of God loose around here."

I noticed then for the first time that nobody had raised his voice above a whisper all day long.

Horn of the Hunter, Robert C. Ruark, 1954

Women on Safari

She always needed a quarter to go to the little girls' room, and now here is a raw stranger, Harry, directing her to the nearest bush and telling her to mind the snakes. This, the girl who wore a Hattie Carnegie frock and a rhinestone hat to ride a camel after a slightly wet evening on the town in Cairo. . . .

"What are you snickering about?" Harry asked.

"Nothing much," I said. "I was just thinking about a dame who is afraid to walk the dogs in Central Park, who is afraid to spend the night alone in a Fifth Avenue penthouse, who spends God knows how much money on girl lunches and at the hairdresser and on her clothes, who would rather be naked than unminked, who wouldn't ride a bus or a subway to save her life, all of a sudden lost out in the African bush with twenty bucks' worth of Indian-made shoddy on her back, fifteen strange cannibals and a strange East African guide, riding in a jeep, looking at lions at close range, weighing a good ten pounds more from dust alone, drinking a hot martini, and going to the john behind a tree while a rank stranger tells her to mind no snakes take a chunk out of her. That is what I am laughing at – Osa Johnson Ruark, girl adventuress."

"I was serious about the snakes," Harry said. "Touch more beer in the bottle. Have it? Knew a girl once was bit on the bottom. Hell's own trouble trying to decide where to put the tourniquet."

Horn of the Hunter, Robert C. Ruark, 1954

"Just before our most exciting adventure"
The real Osa Johnson

An Intoxicating Experience

To Ingeborg Dinesen

Bogani 14/2.1918

. . . I have been down to shoot for a fortnight with Eric Otter on the Tana plains to get buffalo and rhino, which I had not hunted before, and we shot some of both and had a fine safari. It is so beautiful, an absolutely enchanting "romantic" landscape, like Claude Lorrain's, with domed blue mountains, vast brown plains and wide flowing rivers bordered with a wealth of palms and great green trees. But it is fearfully hot there, it is only 3,000 feet – and there is a really hellish plague peculiar to Tana Plains, the small *ticks* that attack you by the million and completely ruin life for you. They are almost invisible, but when you have been out walking in the high grass you look down and see that you are gray with them, worse than the soldiers in the trenches with lice, I think, and it is remarkable that such small creatures can pump you so full of poison and misery; you look as if you had measles all over you and feel as if you are bathed in flame. But there is something about safari life that makes you forget all your sorrows and feel the whole time as if you had drunk half a bottle of champagne, – bubbling over with heartfelt gratitude for being alive. It seems right that human beings should live in the nomad fashion and unnatural to have one's home always in the same place; one only feels really free when one can go in whatever direction one pleases over the plains, get to the river at sundown and pitch one's camp, with the knowledge that one can fall asleep beneath other trees, with another view before one, the next night. I had not sat by a camp fire for three years, and so sitting there again listening to the lions far out in the darkness was like returning to the really true world again, – where I probably once lived 10,000 years ago.

Letters from Africa 1914-31, Isak Dinesen (Karen Blixen)

Big-Game Photography

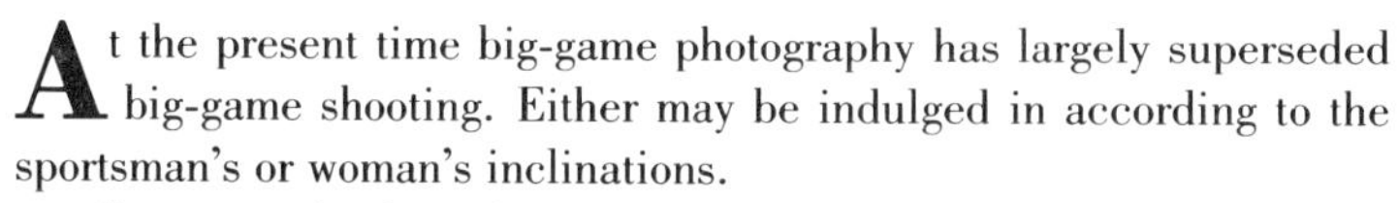

At the present time big-game photography has largely superseded big-game shooting. Either may be indulged in according to the sportsman's or woman's inclinations.

In my youth, the only animals that were photographed were dead animals. This made the problem of animal photography very simple. After your client had shot his trophy, he posed on the dead beast while you clicked the camera. But to-day people are determined to secure pictures of living animals. The animals seldom care to co-operate. A white hunter guiding a photographer has a difficult task.

At first photography was combined with shooting. This never gave good results. A man must use either a camera or a gun – not both. The requirements of the two sports are very different. A sportsman wants his trophy. He cares nothing about weather conditions or the pose of the beast. A photographer must have the sun in a certain position and the animal out in the open so that he can get a good, clear picture. In the early days, picture taking was considered incidental to getting good trophies. I grew up in this tradition and little thought that I would see the day when a good half of all safaris leaving Nairobi would be carrying cameras instead of rifles.

Hunter, J. A. Hunter, 1954

USES FOR AUTOMOBILES IN AFRICA

Pink Flamingoes

We had come down to the Rift Valley by a sandy red road across a high plateau, then up and down through orchard-bushed hills, around a slope of forest to the top of the rift wall where we could look down and see the plain, the heavy forest below the wall, and the long, dried-up edged shine of Lake Manyara rose-coloured at one end with a half million tiny dots that were flamingoes. From there the road dropped steeply along the face of the wall, down into the forest, on to the flatness of the valley, through cultivated patches of green corn, bananas, and trees I did not know the names of, walled thick with forest, past a Hindu's trading store and many huts, over two bridges where clear, fast-flowing streams ran, through more forest, thinning now to open glades, and into a dusty turn-off that led into a deeply rutted, dust-filled track through bushes to the shade of M'utu-Umbu camp.

That night after dinner we heard the flamingoes flighting in the dark. It was like the sound the wings of ducks make as they go over before it is light, but slower, with a steady beat, and multiplied a thousand times.

Green Hills of Africa, Ernest Hemingway, 1936

A Mystery Beyond Words

These things can be told. But there are no words that can tell the hidden spirit of the wilderness, that can reveal its mystery, its melancholy, and its charm. There is delight in the hardy life of the open, in long rides rifle in hand, in the thrill of the fight with dangerous game. Apart from this, yet mingled with it, is the strong attraction of the silent places, of the large tropic moons, and the splendour of the new stars; where the wanderer sees the awful glory of sunrise and sunset in the wide waste spaces of the earth, unworn of man, and changed only by the slow changes of the ages from time everlasting.

African Game Trails, Theodore Roosevelt, 1910

PHILIP PERCIVAL AND GEORGE EASTMAN TALK IT OVER (AT KARO WATERHOLE ON THE KAISOOT DESERT.) PERCIVAL IS ONE OF THE OUTSTANDING BIG GAME HUNTERS OF AFRICA AND A MOST DELIGHTFUL SAFARI COMPANION. MR EASTMAN GETS EVERY BIT OF ENJOYMENT OUT OF SAFARI LIFE, AND TAKES THE KEENEST INTEREST IN CAMP ACTIVITIES.

THE RHYTHM OF AFRICA

Out in the wilds I had learned to beware of abrupt movements. The creatures with which you are dealing there are shy and watchful, they have a talent for evading you when you least expect it. No domestic animal can be as still as a wild animal. The civilized people have lost the aptitude of stillness, and must take lessons in silence from the wild before they are accepted by it. The art of moving gently, without suddenness, is the first to be studied by the hunter, and more so by the hunter with the camera. Hunters cannot have their own way, they must fall in with the wind, and the colours and smells of the landscape, and they must make the tempo of the ensemble their own. Sometimes it repeats a movement over and over again, and they must follow up with it.

When you have caught the rhythm of Africa, you find that it is the same in all her music. What I learned from the game of the country was useful to me in my dealings with the native people.

Out of Africa, Karen Blixen, 1937

Acknowledgements

PICTURE CREDITS

Front cover: *On the Lookout*, Wilhelm Kuhnert (Fine Art Photographs)
Back cover: (Mary Evans Picture Library)
Title page: *Loading stores in New York bound for the Roosevelt Safari, 1909* (Theodore Roosevelt Collection, Harvard College Library)

4-5 *The Wildebeest Migration*, Simon Combes (© The Artist/Clive Holloway Books/Private Collection)
7 *Restless Before the Storm, 1986*, Simon Combes (© The Artist/Clive Holloway Books)
9 *Pitching Camp: Todd in Africa* (Hulton Picture Company)
11 *Great Western Falls, Victoria Falls, 1873*, Thomas Baines (Bridgeman Art Library/Royal Geographical Society)
13 *Underway for Lake Paradise*, Martin Johnson (Martin & Osa Johnson Safari Museum)
12 (Punch)
15 *Near Sudbury, Cape Province*, Thomas Baines (Bridgeman/Royal Geographical Society)
16 (Punch)
17 *Todd in Africa c.1890* (Hulton Picture Company)
18 *The Hunter*, W. J. Hunter (National Archives, Nairobi, Murumbi Collection)
19 *Frederick Selous* (Mary Evans Picture Library)
21 *Ernest Hemingway with Philip Percival* (Percival Collection, Nairobi, from *Safari – A Chronicle of Adventure*, Bartle Bull, Viking Penguin 1988)
23 *In Camp at Night*, W. J. Hunter (National Archives, Nairobi, Murumbi Collection)
24 (Punch)
25 *The Prince of Wales with Denys Finch Hatton* (Cockie Hoogterp/Errol Trzebinski Collection)
27 *Buffaloes Driven to the Edge of the Chasm Opposite Garden Island, Victoria Falls*, Thomas Baines (Bridgeman/Royal Geographical Society)
29 *Raising the Flag*, Kermit Roosevelt
31 *Victoria Falls*, Thomas Baines (Bridgeman/Royal Geographical Society, London)
33 *In Front of Our Home in Tanganyika*, Martin Johnson (Martin & Osa Johnson Safari Museum)
35 *Zebras in Open Country*, Wilhelm Kuhnert (Fine Art Photographs/ Newman & Cooling)
37 *The Roosevelt Safari* (Mary Evans Picture Library)
39 *Tall Shadows*, Simon Combes (© The Greenwich Workshop Inc, Trumbull, Connecticut)
40 (Punch)
41 *Leading the Way*, Martin Johnson (Martin & Osa Johnson Safari Museum)
43 *Greater Kudu*, David Shepherd (© The Artist)
45 *The Real Osa Johnson*, Martin Johnson (Martin & Osa Johnson Safari Museum)
47 *Buffalo and Thorn Tree*, Simon Combes (© The Artist/Private Collection, Nairobi)
49 *Motor Transport in Africa*, Martin Johnson (Martin & Osa Johnson Safari Museum)
51 *Lake or Expansion of a River in Zululand, 1874*, Thomas Baines (Christie's South Kensington)
52 (Punch)
53 *Philip Percival and George Eastman*, Martin Johnson (Martin & Osa Johnson Safari Museum)
55 *On the Lookout*, Wilhelm Kuhnert (Fine Art Photographs)

TEXT CREDITS

Text extracts from the following sources are reprinted with the kind permission of the publishers and copyright holders stated. Should any copyright holder have been inadvertently omitted they should apply to the publishers who will be pleased to credit them in any subsequent editions.

8 Errol Trzebinski, *The Kenya Pioneers* (William Heinemann 1985)
16, 17, 22, 32, 42, 44: Robert C. Ruark: *Horn of the Hunter* (Hutchinson, 1954, reprinted with the permission of the Peters Fraser & Dunlop Group Ltd. Doubleday & Co, USA. © 1952, 1953 by Robert C. Ruark. Reprinted by permission of Harold Matson Company Inc.)
20, 50: Ernest Hemingway, *The Green Hills of Africa* (Jonathan Cape, the Estate of Ernest Hemingway, copyright 1935 Charles Scribner's Sons; renewal © 1963 by Mary Hemingway)
26, 54: Karen Blixen, *Out of Africa* (Random House, 1937)
30 Isak Dinesen, *Shadows in the Grass* (Random House Inc, USA)
46 Isak Dinesen, *Letters from Africa 1914-31* (© 1981 University of Chicago)
(© Runstedlund Foundation for all Karen Blixen alias Isak Dinesen)
48 J.A. Hunter, *Hunter* (Hamish Hamilton, 1952, reprinted with the permission of the Peters Fraser & Dunlop Group Ltd.)

First published in Great Britain 1991 by
PAVILION BOOKS LIMITED
196 Shaftesbury Avenue, London WC2H 8JL

Designed by Andrew Barron & Collis Clements Associates

A CIP catalogue record for this book is available from the British Library

ISBN 1-85145-799-2

Printed and bound in Scotland by Eagle Colour Books